A MOTHER'S
WISDOM

written & illustrated by
Anne Marie Walsh

SATURN PRESS, INC.

Library Of Congress Catalog Card Number: 96-069573

ISBN 1-885843-01-1

FIRST EDITION

Published by Saturn Press, Inc.
17639 Foxborough La.
Boca Raton, Florida 33496

Contents

Acknowledgements

Special thanks to Tom and Matthew for being the greatest kids a mother could wish for. Major thanks to Tom who played a critical part in the design and layout of this book. Tom's computer wisdom not only helped with the completion of this book, he also brought Mom into the computer age. Thanks to Teny and Sylvia for your words of wisdom. To my Mother, I only wish you were still here to see that I did learn from you. Extra special thanks to Pat. Thank you for your love, support, understanding, and gentle guidance.

Foreword

Over the last 30 years, we, as parents, started turning away from our own common sense feelings of how to raise children and instead relied on professionals to guide our way. The overcrowded shelves in the parenting section of book stores and libraries attest to this trend. Although so many of these professional texts are rich with wisdom and have certainly helped many, there is something missing . . . a parent's voice. What about the knowledge that comes from having raised children? Could there be a longer on-the-job-training program or more intense internship?

Bringing children into the world and teaching them to be sensitive and productive human beings is the most difficult of jobs. Forget politicians and professional athletes; their jobs dim when compared to the daily responsibilities of mothers and fathers. Parents have the important job. Passing your knowledge onto your children so that they can do it better than you did is an intimidating task.

A Mother's Wisdom is a wonderful contribution at a time when many of us are wondering if we have gone morally and ethically adrift. It is a powerful reminder that when it comes to raising children, true knowing comes not from the accumulation of degrees but from patience, common sense, and love.

Kathy Levinson, Ph.D.
Author of *Raising Sensitive Children
When the World Seems So Crazy*

Introduction

"Boy have times changed since I was a child," is an expression I remember hearing throughout my childhood. I find myself thinking about this age-old expression more and more, notably since becoming a parent myself. I don't think any generation of children has been exposed to the degree of sex and violence our children are today. The generation of children we are raising now are facing things we never would have imagined when we were their age. I am sure the senior citizens of today are as bewildered as we parents are as to what is going on with our nation's children.

Since I was a child I have been an observer of people. I have noticed over the years how parenting has changed from one generation to another.

Some of the changes are good but many negatively affect our children. Too often, people rely on outside sources to raise their children, instead of trusting their natural instincts. We are inundated with advice from thousands of different sources, from professional people to toy manufacturers, all proclaiming what they think is good for our children. What's a parent to do?

The only sensible answer is A Mother's Wisdom . . . good old common sense. I hope this little book of hints will help parents find some logical solutions to the day-to-day problems we all face.

Anne Marie Walsh

DOING THE RIGHT THING

Don't make promises you can't keep. Teach your children the value of your word. When you promise your children something, keep your end of the bargain.

★

Instill in your children the idea that all dreams are possible. Individuals who are willing to work hard without giving up can attain their goals.

★

Always let your child know you stand behind him or her, but before you jump to make excuses for your child, find out the whole story.

Defend your children when you know they are right.

★

"Oh shh . . . sugar!" I always thought my mother was silly to use that expression, but now I see she was teaching us to express frustration without cursing. Children learn by example. If you use bad language, you can be sure they will use it too.

★

Teach your children to be individuals.
Help them to believe in themselves.

★

Let your children see you work hard.

Never argue with friends, neighbors, or your
guests in front of your children.

★

Tell your children there is nothing wrong
with walking away from a fight.

★

Never ask your child to lie for you and always
tell the truth in front of your children.

★

Teach your children right from wrong
at an early age.

★

You can never hug, kiss, or praise your child enough.

If you are a coach, remember it's only a game and the players are only children. Have fun, don't push too hard. If you remember to have fun, the kids on your team will always look up to you.

Never bribe your children!

Perfection is a heavy burden to place on young shoulders. Tell your children you simply want them to do the best they can.

Borrowing is a bad habit. If your child borrows money or any other item, make sure he or she returns it promptly.

★

Help your children to be truthful, not only
with other people but with themselves.

★

Never argue with your child in front of his or her friends.
It's embarrassing. Ask your child to join you in another
room or wait until you are alone with your child.

★

Teach your children to be punctual and that
it is rude to keep people waiting.

★

Teach your children the importance of dressing appropriately for religious services, school, field trips, and company.

One of the most interesting aspects of parenthood is watching your child become a unique and separate individual from you with his or her own beliefs and ideals. Express your own beliefs and opinions to your child, but don't force him or her to conform to your way of thinking.

If a neighbor, friend, or teacher tells you that your child is up to something, don't take the attitude "not my child." Maybe that person is seeing things that you're not.

Teach your children to stand when they are
being introduced to someone.

★

We are surrounded by opportunities to teach
our little ones the importance of manners and
respect for elders such as giving up your seat to
an older person while riding a bus or train.

★

Want phrases like "thank you," "you're welcome,"
"please," and "excuse me" to become second nature
to your children? Use them in your home.

Did you ever notice that some children eat like they were raised by wolves? They gobble down their food and talk with their mouths full? Teach your child proper table manners.

★

Insist your son remove his hat when entering a building.

★

When you see one of your friends stressed to the limit and unable to cope, offer to watch his or her children for a few hours.

We all cringe at children who ask every visitor to their home, "Did you bring me something?" Teach your children to avoid this rude and awkward question.

★

If you have an argument in the presence of your children and you know you were wrong, let your children see you apologize.

★

Have you ever observed the behavior of some parents at a Little League game? If your child doesn't make the team, don't pull strings. Let it go.

★

Most children want to be accepted; being different is hard. Encourage your children to get to know a gifted child or a child with a learning disability before they label them "stupid" or "nerd." Most kids have at least one thing in common.

When your children attend a party, make sure
they personally thank the host and hostess.

★

Teach your children to behave properly in a theater.
Explain how talking and getting out of their seats
annoys the people who are there to enjoy the show.

★

When your child receives a gift, no matter what it is,
make sure he or she writes a thank-you note.

Be aware that you could be taking advantage of a friend
or neighbor's hospitality. When your child spends time
at a friend's home, make sure you reciprocate.

★

Let your children know the value of their possessions
from toys to clothing. This helps your children learn
responsibility. They are less likely to lose things
if they know their possessions' worth.

★

Find a place in your home for your children to keep their
toys. Teach them organization at a young age; don't
allow toys scattered all over your home.

★

On a beautiful day, don't let your children sit and watch television or play video games. Go outside. There is so much to explore and learn.

At a certain age some children become very modest. Respect your children's feelings and don't get insulted if they ask you to leave the room.

★

Giving your child the silent treatment is a manipulation and not responsible parenting. Ask yourself is this something you would want your child to copy?

★

Never compare your children to anyone. Hearing "you're not as smart as your brother" can be devastating to a child.

LEARNING AND EDUCATION

★

Everything you do with your child can be a learning experience. Something as simple as flying a kite can turn into a lesson on Ben Franklin and electricity.

If you have a major concern about your child and have trouble working it out, reach out. Go see his or her teacher, principal, or school psychologist for suggestions.

When you are willing to accept mediocre work from your children, don't be surprised if that's what you get.

Competition can teach life skills. Show your child how to win with grace and lose with dignity.

Stress to your children the importance of an education.

Do not expect your children's school to teach morals and values. Every family weaves a unique pattern of beliefs and values, a familial moral code. Only you can determine what that pattern should be.

★

Take time to read to your children every day.

★

While it is important for everyone in the family to have responsibilities, children should know that going to school is the most important thing they do.

Children learn to speak better and to use proper English if you read to them.

★

Show your child how to set a table for a meal. If you're not sure how to do it properly, get a book on etiquette.

★

When a teacher tells you that your child is working up to potential but you know your child can achieve more, speak up! Who knows your child better?

Teach your children self-control and restraint
at a young age.

★

Go to open school night at your child's school.
Even if you have to change your plans.

★

Keep lots of books and magazines in your home.
Make sure your children see you reading!

★

Go to your children's plays and concerts; take lots of pictures and videos. Let them know how proud you are, even if they make mistakes.

Bet you can't guess who has the most rights in school?
Nope. It's you.

★

Make sure you see your children's finished homework every
night. Keep track of what they are doing in school.

★

If your child has trouble taking notes at school, buy him or
her a new notebook and show your child how it's done.

Don't discourage your child from studying with other children. Some children learn better in a group. Just make sure he or she knows the material afterwards.

If you see your child's grades slipping, call the teacher immediately and request a conference.

Help your children with their handwriting. People take notice of neat legible penmanship in adults.

Encourage your children to stick with what they have
started. If you let them quit before trying hard
you're sending the wrong message.

Knowing how to ask a good question is an art form because
the more we ask the more we learn. Encourage your
children to learn by asking questions!

Encourage your child to read the newspaper every day.
Share the comics and talk about the latest current events.

If your child suddenly seems anxious and tense, find out what is going on. Don't waste time. A visit to his or her teacher could shed some light on the problem.

★

If your child is being hit or bullied by another child at school or on the bus, get in touch with the principal and explain the problem. Usually, when an authority figure intervenes, the action stops.

★

You have every right to know what is in your child's school file. All you need to do is ask. The same holds true for your child's medical records.

★

Make sure your child gets enough sleep. A tired child will not learn well.

Have you ever been the new kid on the block? Make moving to a new neighborhood and new school as painless as possible. Before you move, check out the school your children will be attending. Introduce yourself to the principal and don't be afraid to ask questions.

Insist that children be respectful to teachers and all school personnel.

Ask your child's teacher to give more challenging work when your child seems bored with schoolwork or is finishing before anyone else.

All children have at least one special talent. Help your
children to use their strengths to improve on
their weaknesses.

★

When your children are athletically involved, insist that
they keep up with their school work. The glory
days go by very quickly.

★

If you never finished high school or college, wouldn't
it be a great example for your children to see
you get your diploma?

★

Play hide and seek with your little ones and always let them find you.

Children need time to relax and just be children. Too often they are rushed to grow up. It's very easy to overload your children with afterschool activities. Keep it simple: a music lesson, sports practice, and one game a week should keep them busy.

★

When you know your child will not be attending college, encourage him or her to learn a trade or skill.

★

Like remind your child that like the word "like" doesn't belong in like every sentence. Like okay?

America, the great melting pot, affords us the opportunity to *expose* our children to many different cultures. Try some exotic foods, foreign films, and cultural exhibits.

★

Let your children know that most movies and television shows are fiction. Explain the difference between real and make-believe.

★

Most children believe the commercials they see on television are true. Explain to them that people receive enormous amounts of money to make products look good so consumers will buy them.

★

Encourage your children to play a musical instrument. It fosters self-discipline, creativity, and it's great for the soul!

Teach your children to never open a closed door without first knocking and to never open somebody's front door unless invited to do so.

★

"Do unto others as you would have them do unto you" are words we can all live by no matter what our religion. Teach your children to treat people the way they would like people to treat them in return.

★

Never put anyone down in front of your children, no matter how angry you are.

Educational television can bring the arts, geography. . .
the world, into our living rooms. Encourage your children
to watch educational shows on television.

★

If you have a special craft or talent, share
it with your children.

★

Take your children out at night to look at the stars. Make
a game of it; see who can find the most constellations.
Pick up an astronomy book to help you identify
stars, planets, and constellations.

Children should know how to handle money. Open a bank account for them and encourage them to save.

★

A father teaches his son respect for women by respecting his child's mother. The same goes for mother and daughter.

SAFE AND SOUND

★

If your child has a security blanket, why argue that they give it up? Think about it, what is your security blanket?

Know where your children are at all times.

★

Never be afraid to seek professional help for your children.

★

On a Saturday night I saw a toddler with his parents in the theater watching an R-rated, blow 'em up, kill everybody movie. The image of that little child staring up at those graphic scenes makes me uncomfortable to this day. Young children do not have the ability to know the difference between make-believe danger and the real thing.

Illegal drugs do not belong in your home. Ever.

Stop your child immediately if you see him or her being cruel to an animal. This behavior may be more serious than mischievous and may warrant a consultation with your family physician or local psychologist.

★

Try to limit junk and fast foods in your children's diet. Keep healthy snacks on hand.

★

Be concerned when a healthy child unexpectedly starts to stutter. This may warrant a consultation with your family doctor.

★

Point out the word DANGER to your little ones and make sure they know what it means.

Even children need to feel comfortable and to trust
their doctor. Find a doctor who is "kid friendly."

Prepare your child if he or she is getting a shot at the
doctor's office. Don't say it doesn't hurt if it will but try
not to frighten your child unnecessarily. Discuss how
they can distract themselves by counting down
from 100 or humming a favorite song.

Teach your children to cover their mouths
when they cough or sneeze.

Keep all medications on a top shelf, far out of your children's reach, in a locked medicine chest. Make sure all medications are clearly labeled and in child-proof containers. It only takes a second for disaster to occur.

★

As important as dentists are, few people, including children like to go see them. They have those metal poker things and all those scary gadgets hanging over the chair. Still, children who learn to take care of their teeth at an early age will be very thankful later on.

★

Whether you're in a store or just walking down the street, point out words on signs to your children. Start with easy safety words such as stop, go, in, out, up, down, and exit. It will amaze you how fast your child will learn to pick up these words. This is a good start to reading.

Many parents complain that their children's eating habits are atrocious. Some children eat like birds while others seem like garbage compactors. However, if you notice a dramatic gain or loss of weight in your child get him or her checked by your doctor.

Beware the "Weekday Flu." The symptoms? Your child says he or she is sick every morning on school days but is fine on the weekend. Something is wrong; find out the cause of this weekday illness.

Don't fool around with high fevers, get medical help.
It's not worth taking a risk with your child's health.

★

If your child has a disability, never let him or her give
up. Spiritual strength and courage can help meet
the challenge. If you can't handle all the demands
alone, enlist family and friends to help you both.

★

Talk to your daughter about menstruation before she
gets her period. If you need help, there are many
books available on this subject.

Follow your instincts when it comes to your children's health. Too many young parents allow themselves to be "bullied" by pediatricians who tell them, "Oh, it's nothing," when instinctively the parents KNOW something is very wrong with their child.

Allow your children to attend a wake or funeral only if they want to. Prepare them and tell them what to expect. Be there to help them through these first experiences with death.

Young children and balloons or marbles don't mix. With a natural curiosity to taste and put things in their mouths, many a young child has choked. Be careful.

★

If your child tells you that someone has touched or spoken to him or her inappropriately, never dismiss it. Operate on the side of safety and investigate.

★

If you're apprehensive about buying toy guns for your children then don't. There are many other toys they can enjoy.

★

Something is wrong if your child is constantly getting into fights. Get a handle on this problem and find out why your child is so angry.

When I was a teenager I had a great arrangement
with my parents. I called them when I got to
my friend's house and then I called if I went
someplace else. My parents relaxed because they
always knew where to find me, and I had fun.

Your children should know what to do if they get lost.
For instance, if your children get separated from you at
the mall, instruct them to walk up to another mother
with children or to approach a security guard.

In my family, we always had a "lost plan." Every time we went to a park or carnival, my father picked a "landmark" and said to go there if we got separated and he would meet me there.

★

If your child is going to a sleep-over, make sure the parents of the host or hostess will be home and that your child is going to be supervised.

★

Introduce yourself to the parents of children your kids are spending a good amount of time with.

Check on your child before you go to sleep. Make sure your house is secure and each outside door is locked.

★

When was the last time you checked the smoke alarm in your house?

★

Never let your children walk home alone at night. Make sure you are there to pick them up.

★

As soon as your children start to talk, begin teaching them their name, address, phone number, and what town and state they live in.

Make sure your children can reach a telephone. Teach them how to dial 911 and what to say in an emergency. Role play!

★

Teach your children to never let a stranger on the phone know they are home alone.

★

If your child is fighting with a friend, don't step in unless it gets physical.

★

If your children are home alone, instruct them to never open the door for anyone except you.

We live in a dangerous era. Don't let your child out of your sight in a public place for one second. If a stranger approaches your child and you are not in sight have your child yell LOUDLY, "I don't know you. I want my mother!!!" Nowadays that should get attention FAST.

Never put your children's names on the outside of their clothing, school bag, or lunch box. Young children can get confused if it appears that a "stranger" knows their name.

No matter how many times you drill it into their heads, children are still going to help that stranger find the lost puppy. Close supervision is the best form of protection.

Should a stranger stop your child for directions, make sure that he or she knows to stand far away from the car. If they don't feel safe with the situation, instruct them to get away as quickly as possible.

A recipe for disaster: children and guns. Make sure your firearms and the bullets are locked separately and out of your children's reach.

Selecting a safe and responsible day care center is an important decision that should never be made quickly. Spend time observing and always get several references. Most importantly, follow your intuition about the center's ability to properly care for your child.

Put matches and lighters far out of reach from little hands.

Choose carefully when selecting a baby-sitter for your children. Many people don't think twice about entrusting care of their most precious treasure to an inexperienced 13-year-old child who will be paid less than minimum wage.

Children cannot learn soon enough that guns in the wrong hands are deadly. If they find themselves around an individual with a gun they should leave immediately and report the incident to you.

Teach your child the right way to cross a busy street.

Have you ever seen the news program that illustrates what can happen in an accident to children when they are not wearing their seat belts or properly secured in their car seat? It's chilling.

★

I hate to be the Grinch who stole everyone's good time but many children have gotten seriously and permanently injured because they weren't wearing helmets while riding their bikes or rollerblading. For the same reasons you "buckle up," put those helmets on.

Even if you just have to run inside the store for a second, do not leave a small child alone in a car. The potential for danger is very real.

Teach your children how to safely play with pets and to keep away from animals they don't know.

Know where your little ones are when you are opening the oven door or cooking on the stove. Their natural curiosity could cost them serious injury or worse.

Don't let your children swim at an unprotected
beach or lake.

★

Sometimes, children don't realize how rough they
are playing. Explain how rough play can lead
to someone getting seriously hurt.

★

Never let your children walk around with large sums
of money. Explain that flashing money around
could tempt someone to steal it.

"Feet first!" Make sure your children know to jump feet first into shallow or unfamiliar water. Many, many children have sustained spinal cord injuries because they dove head first into shallow water or struck a concealed object.

A dryer is a tempting but dangerous hiding place. Keep the dryer door closed at all times.

When buying a sleeping bag, make sure the tag says flame resistant.

While most of us will never know the terror of a house fire, those who have survived one will never forget. Every member of the family should know what to do in case of a fire. If you want to make a lasting impression on your little ones, take them to your local firehouse or have a firefighter inspect your home.

★

Most children love the water but they must learn to respect it. Teach water safety early and consistently.

★

Never let your children play on elevators or escalators.

★

Many good friendships have ended after parents got involved in their children's fights. The children make up but the parents remain enemies. Stay out of your children's quarrels unless it gets rough.

Strap your child into the grocery cart when food shopping.
In the time it takes for you to select a carton of eggs your
child could stand up and fall out of the cart. A good
rule of thumb is to constantly keep one of your
hands on the cart at all times.

Have a special family password. If a stranger confronts your
child and the person can't give the password, your child
should realize that this person is not being truthful.

SURVIVING YOUR TEENAGER

★

Puberty is a roller coaster ride.
Hold on, you will get through it!

When you are a child it is hard to resist thinking and behaving like everybody else. There is always the risk that friends will turn away or worse, people will think you are weird. Support your children when they dare to defend their beliefs.

★

We all read newspapers and know that teenagers mistakenly believe they can take foolish risks and still cheat death. You can't be with your children every minute but you can point out reckless behavior when you see it. When you see a wise guy run a red light ask your child what could have happened.

★

Never let your children hang out without a purpose. Open your home to your children's friends, make some popcorn, and rent a video.

Just because "everyone is doing it" does not mean your child has to follow the crowd. Teach him or her to be a leader, not a follower.

★

If you are not comfortable with your child going someplace, or going with a certain group of people, trust your instincts.

★

Although it may feel like yesterday since you were 16, act your age in front of your teenager's friends.

Be honest. If you don't like one of your child's friends, let him or her know why you feel this way.

★

Let your teenagers know that they can get pregnant the first time.

★

Be aware of the lure of temptation. Don't allow your teenager to entertain friends when you're not home. Explain to your child why you don't want anyone to visit.

Teenagers and telephones, need I say more? Yelling won't get your teenager off the phone any sooner but it will raise your blood pressure. Consider investing in call-waiting.

You should be your child's source of information on serious topics such as abortion and condoms. These two subjects are in the news every day and only you can explain your moral position as well as offering factual information.

When you go out and leave your car at home, take your car keys with you. Don't leave temptation sitting in your driveway.

Never serve alcoholic beverages to a minor.

★

When your children are in high school, keep in touch with their teachers and school work. Your children need to know you still care just as much about them and their schoolwork as you did in the younger years.

★

If you think your teenager is involved in things you disapprove of, confront him or her. Ignoring the situation won't make it go away and may give your teen the impression that you don't care.

★

If your child has a weight problem, encourage; never tease. Go on a diet together or make sure you prepare meals to help him or her stick to a diet.

One of the fastest growing groups infected with AIDS in our country is teenagers. Their cavalier "won't happen to me" attitude can cost them dearly. Don't be afraid to talk about this subject and to stress abstinence.

In the 60s hitchhiking was considered cool and an acceptable way for teenagers to get around (as long as your parents didn't know about it). Today it can be downright deadly.

DISCIPLINE WITH A HEART

★

Verbal abuse can be just as harmful as physical abuse. Never, ever tell your children they are stupid, ugly, or worthless.

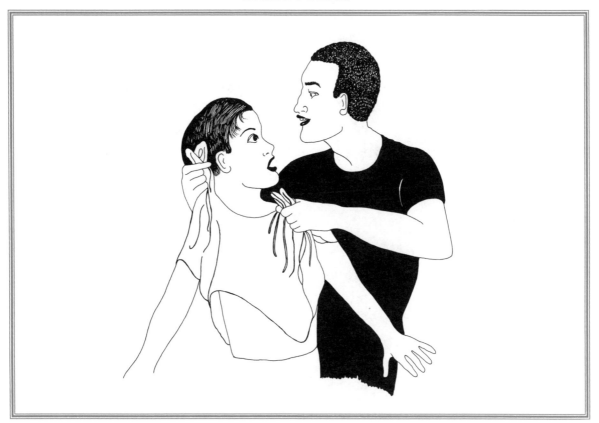

The first time you walk into your living room and see the walls covered in crayon, you will realize one of the most important rules of parenthood is no matter what happens, keep your sense of humor. Someday your children will be all grown and you'll find yourself wishing they were young enough to color your living room again.

★

Hitting your children sends them the message
that it is okay to hit others.

★

Your children need structure in their lives.
A set bedtime is important.

Though they probably won't admit it, structure and rules provide your children with a sense of security. Set rules that your children can abide by, then stick to them.

★

Explain to your children the importance of respecting other people's property. Graffiti and vandalism are not just mischievous. They are crimes. If you have to, draw analogies. "How would you feel if we all woke up tomorrow and the outside of our house or car was spray-painted?"

At a young age, teach your children the concept of good citizenship. We must obey the laws and keep our communities clean. Being a good citizen includes never littering.

It is great to be your child's friend but there are times when you have to be firm. Your child wants you to be in charge.

Never tell a child to shut up. "Please be quiet" or "hush" sounds so much nicer.

If you punish your child, stick to your guns. Children
need to know what you expect from them.

★

When you know your child is bullying another child
because he or she is different, put a stop to it.
Children learn tolerance at home.

★

Have a time-out place in your home. Sometimes
a child needs a safe spot to calm down.

★

Sometimes adults have to remind themselves that they were once children. Go back in your memory, put yourself in your child's shoes, you might remember what your child is feeling.

My mother had this unexplainable way of knowing when I or any of my brothers was lying. With her big brown eyes in a piercing stare, we would know our cover was blown and there would be "trouble" to pay. Encourage your children to tell the truth and to not be afraid to "fess up" when they have done wrong.

Don't discipline your child publicly. Take your child into another room or outside to avoid embarrassment to you both.

If your child screams at you, don't scream back. A gentle reply can keep things in perspective.

★

I had a curfew when I was a kid and I hated it. All my friends got to stay out after dark but not me. Now I realize that my parents were right. Children should have a set curfew and you should enforce it.

★

Cheaters never prosper. Whether in a game or contest, your child should never cheat to win. If you know your child won a prize due to cheating, insist he or she return the award. It is a good exercise in humility.

Peer pressure is alive and well.
Teach your children the difference
between right and wrong and
that you expect them to do
the right thing.

Respect your child's privacy. If you happen to find
something, try not to immediately pounce on him
or her. Cool down first, then go on to
explore the situation rationally.

There is a special monitoring device on all television
sets . . . the "off" button. Put a limit on television time.
Know what your children are watching and if
you don't approve, turn it off.

FAMILY LIFE

★

Teach your children how to do laundry and how to fold and put it away.

When you're having a bad day, don't take it out
on your children. It's not their fault.

★

As sad as it is, death is an inevitable part of our world. In
some households death is never spoken of and this just
creates fear of the unknown. When your children are young,
speak about death as a natural part of the cycle of life.

★

Never be afraid to let your children see you cry.

Play cards or teach your children to play a board game.
It's a good time for getting to know each other.

★

Enough cannot be said about the importance of family pets
and the great opportunity they provide to teach your
children how to love and care for other living things.

★

Encourage your child to express his or her point of view,
even if it differs from yours. You may even find
yourself seeing things differently and
understanding your child better.

Be serious about parenting but don't be a serious parent.

Children need to learn that they cannot have everything, and that accumulating things can be an empty experience. Going into debt so your children can keep up with the crowd is foolish. If you can't afford something, explain it to your children. If you can afford it but still don't like the idea of $150 sneakers, say so!

If your child just has to have those $150 sneakers and you can't or won't buy them, let your child choose to earn the money.

Trust is a hard thing to get back once it is lost. Both parent and child have to work hard at keeping each other's trust.

★

When you hug and kiss your children often, don't be surprised if they hug or kiss you in front of their friends.

★

When you see your child grow frustrated with something, have the child stop and relax. Then step in to give advice or a helping hand if necessary.

For most adults, snowstorms are a big bother — shoveling snow and scraping off the windshield at seven in the morning. Bundle everybody up and have a ball. Make angels in the snow, catch snowflakes on your tongue, build a snowman!

Take your children to a playground. Go on the swings, seesaw, slide, and monkey bars with them. Get down to their level, if only for a few minutes. HAVE FUN!

★

Although they may like it, do children really need a television, VCR, and a telephone in their rooms?

★

There is no reason why boys and girls cannot play together and have a good time. Don't make an issue of it and never tease.

Holidays offer the opportunity to create exciting and treasured memories for you and your children. Pass on any family traditions you have to your children. If you don't have any family customs, start your own.

★

Tell your children interesting little stories about when you were pregnant with them. Children also love to hear about when they were infants and toddlers.

★

Your home should be a peaceful, happy environment for your children. Don't bring the office or any other pressure home to disrupt your family.

★

Show your children that books are a way of opening a world of creativity and imagination. Get each child a library card and visit the library often.

If you don't have family living nearby, encourage your children to be pen pals with their cousins or other relatives. This can be a fun way to keep in touch and to improve reading and writing skills.

★

Show your children any family heirlooms you may have inherited. Let them know the value of your treasure. Not in terms of money, but in the intangible sentimental value the items have for you.

★

Share a good joke or funny story with your family at dinner time. Go around the table and have everyone do the same.

Encourage your children to talk to you about their feelings.
Let them express joy, anger, fear, and sadness.
Never dismiss their feelings or say something like,
"You have nothing to be sad about."

★

When children see their parents laughing and having
fun together, it can be very reassuring to them.

★

If a divorce is inevitable, there is one last promise you must
make with your spouse: to never, under any circumstances,
put your children in the middle of your battles.

★

Let your children know about their ancestry. Tell them from what country their ancestors came, when they came, and how they got to this country. Share any old photos, letters, documents, and special stories you may have.

A pet's death can be as traumatic as a family member's death. Holding a funeral can ease the pain.
Don't forget a eulogy.

★

We have many family rituals that we hold dear. Every so often my husband will take the boys to the cemetery to pay respects to a grandfather they never met. The scene at the grave is sincere but not gloomy because they'll share a joke or a family story. In those moments, past meets present and the importance of family is rejuvenated once again.

Fill your house with photographs. Put them everywhere including the bathroom!

★

When your child achieves a major accomplishment, put signs all over your home to congratulate him or her. Show how proud you are.

★

It may be inconvenient and the dinner table too small but allow your child to invite their friends to eat over. A new face at the table creates new conversation, new stories, another way to share quality time with your children.

★

If your children want to play with toys traditional to the opposite sex, don't overreact, let them play with the toy.

Give your child a spiritual foundation.

★

I have friends who still have to pick up their husband's dirty socks. Start young and teach your children to pick up their clothes. Make sure they know where to find the hamper.

★

A few years ago my brother handed me a letter I wrote to Santa when I was a little girl. The sloppy handwriting and childish requests were a sweet reminder of my childhood. Save your children's art work, poetry, and hand-made cards.

The person who said "Children should be seen and not heard" probably put coal in their children's stockings too. Of course children should be heard and seen and cherished. They are our greatest gift and our biggest accomplishment.

★

Most teens will not leave for college or move out on their own still using a night light, so if your young child insists on a night light at bedtime, leave it on. The light is soothing and your child will outgrow the need.

★

Work side by side in the garden, inspire a love of nature in your children. Teach how to plant flowers and vegetables and how to care for them.

Don't make your dinner table a war zone. When your
children don't want to eat something, ignore it.
They will eat enough to get by and you'll all
enjoy the meal if food is not an issue.

★

Talk to your children about how it was when you were
growing up. Tell them stories about their grandparents,
aunts, and uncles. This gives them a sense of roots and
where they come from. It also sends a message of
permanence to your children. We have always
been a family and we always will be.

Be sensitive about the nickname you give to a child. Would you want to be called Lumpy for the rest of your life?

★

Adopted children may have lots of questions about their biological family. It doesn't mean they love you any less. Remember, parenthood is born in the heart.

★

If you're starting to "lose it" with your child, walk away for a few moments. Calm down and find your patience before you do or say something you may regret.

Create a warm, comfortable feeling in your home.
A place your children love to come home to.
A home isn't about the possessions filling it up. It's not
about how many televisions you have or brand-new
furniture. It's about that intangible feeling of peace
and belonging. A sense of relief at the end of the
day when you can just be who you are and
loved for who you are.